The
People's
Bible

It is impossible to overestimate the significance of the Bible to the language and cultures of the English-speaking world. Martyn Payne's The People's Bible *will help teachers and young people to explore the richness of the language, history and message of the Bible in a lively and engaging way. It is a must to help schools celebrate the Bible in English in the year 2011.*

Ann Holt OBE
Director of Programme, Bible Society

An inspiring and creative publication for 2011 and beyond, packed with information and activities that I would recommend to all primary school teachers, RE advisers and ITT providers.

Juliet Lyal
Primary Vice-Chair of NATRE (National Association of Teachers of RE);
group leader of St Albans RE Teachers Together (SARETT)

Martyn Payne calls the publishing of the Bible in English a revolution and after reading this book you realise just how right he is. Packed full of fascinating facts and activity ideas, the children in your school will be inspired.

Lisa Fenton
Senior Adviser to Schools,
Blackburn Diocesan Board of Education

A handy treasure chest for teachers wanting to extend their own knowledge and understanding of the Bible, its translation and transmission, with lots of useful resource material for challenging classroom activities.

Heather Farr
Senior Adviser, Religious Education,
Staffordshire School Improvement Division

The
People's
Bible

A practical handbook of information and cross-curricular activities for primary school teachers to celebrate the Bible in English and mark the 400th anniversary of the King James Version

Martyn Payne

*BRF wishes to acknowledge, with thanks, the grant assistance from
The Drummond Trust, 3 Pitt Terrace, Sterling,
which has made the publication of this book possible.*

Published by
The Bible Reading Fellowship
15 The Chambers, Vineyard
Abingdon OX14 3FE
United Kingdom
Tel: +44 (0)1865 319700
Email: enquiries@brf.org.uk
Website: www.brf.org.uk
BRF is a Registered Charity

ISBN 978 1 84101 852 2
First published 2010
10 9 8 7 6 5 4 3 2 1 0
All rights reserved

Acknowledgments
Extracts from the Authorised Version of the Bible (The King James Bible), the rights in which
are vested in the Crown, are reproduced by permission of the Crown's Patentee, Cambridge
University Press.

Scripture quotations marked (CEV) are from the Contemporary English Version published by
The Bible Societies/HarperCollins Publishers, copyright © 1991, 1992, 1995 American Bible
Society.

Scripture quotations from THE MESSAGE. Copyright © by Eugene H. Peterson 1993, 1994,
1995. Used by permission of NavPress Publishing Group.

A catalogue record for this book is available from the British Library

Printed in Singapore by Craft Print International Ltd

Contents

Foreword

The King James Bible of 1611 is celebrated as the pinnacle of the first Bibles to be produced in English. Written in the language of the age of Shakespeare, it combined poetic expression with a concern for communicating meaning. *The People's Bible* captures the excitement that our forbears must have felt to have the Bible available in English in an easy accessible form. To our culture, which is accustomed to books, the innovation of the Bible in English is difficult to imagine: *The People's Bible* likens it to the arrival of the Internet.

This resource will help teachers and pupils to celebrate this significant event in history, an event that affected language, politics, literature, religion, art and daily life. *The People's Bible* details some of those effects, providing activities that encourage pupils to explore them further. The activities help pupils to engage with the Bible in ways that make this resource useful in RE, History and English.

The People's Bible looks at the influence of the Bible on the development of the English language, its spelling and expression. Thus, pupils are enabled to see the roots of English in the past and understand how the Bible has enriched their language.

The political influence of the Bible is explored by looking at its role in transforming people's aspirations within a changing society. Illustrations are taken from the English Civil War and the abolition of the slave trade, through to recent movements such as the 'Drop the Debt' campaign.

All in all, this book will help schools to celebrate the 400th anniversary of the King James Bible in 2011, but it will also stand as a very helpful resource for many years to come.

Margaret Cooling, INSET specialist and author of over 50 books on RE and Collective Worship

What is all the fuss about?

To pick up a copy of the King James Version of the Bible and open its double-columned pages may not seem like anything special to us today, but 400 years ago, in 1611, doing just this was nothing short of a revolution. This translation of the Bible into the contemporary English of the day was 'authorised' by King James I of England and was dedicated to him: hence it is also known as the Authorised Bible. This English Bible for the people opened up a whole new world of possibilities and led to changes in thinking that shaped the course of history and the culture of the Western world. This one book has left a lasting legacy right up to the present day.

Just imagine: being able to read the Bible in your own language of English was like... the first time our generation logged on to the Internet. Suddenly a whole new world of information and ideas was at its fingertips.

It was like... the first time our generation used an iPhone to speak to and even see friends and relatives overseas. Suddenly a whole new world of communications and contacts was available at the touch of a series of numbers.

It was like... the first time our generation, while watching live TV, was able to influence the outcome of events by pressing a red button. Suddenly a whole new world of influence and power could be accessed by ordinary men and women, who until then had received everything second-hand and at a disabling distance.

Just imagine it! Until English translations of the Bible gradually became available over the 16th century, culminating in the publication of the King James Version in 1611, the people of this country had no direct access to the stories, truths and power of this most influential of books. As most people couldn't read then, they received the Bible predigested by those with the education and knowledge to read it in Greek or Latin. But now any English-speaker could understand the Bible, and with that understanding came the power to decide for themselves what the Bible meant for them and how it would shape their lives, their communities and their whole culture. Christianity throughout the British Isles and the English-speaking world was going to change—with consequences for the whole world.

The translation of the Bible into the English-speaking people's common language was a moment in history that sent shockwaves around the world. It shaped whole nations, influenced whole cultures and brought to birth an unprecedented global response to the Christian faith in the founding of hospitals and schools, churches and charities, philosophies and political movements, as well as the creation of countless works of art, literature and music, which has been unstoppable. The Bible became something that was open to all people, not just the educated and the clergy. The record of God's story in the pages of scripture became at last the people's Bible, whose anniversary we celebrate in 2011.

Activity suggestions

1. Pick up a copy of the King James Version of the Bible and hold it in your hands for a few minutes before opening it. Imagine what it felt like for the ordinary people of your city, town or village in 1611 to have this book available in their own language. Over the previous 100 years, English translations had been gradually appearing, but now people were able to own a copy at home, legally and openly.

   Can you suggest what feelings would be going through those people's minds? What hopes and what possibilities would they be thinking about?

   Now open a version of the Bible in a different language and read a short passage. This was how the Bible sounded to most people before an English version appeared. Until this moment in history, only trained clergy and academics could have understood it.

Reproduced with permission from *The People's Bible* published by BRF 2010 (978 1 84101 852 2) www.barnabasinschools.org.uk

What do you think it felt like for a person in those days to be able to hear the Bible read out loud in English, perhaps even in their own homes? What could that person now do that couldn't have been done before?

2. Place your King James Version next to an iPhone or laptop. Consider what parallels you can draw between these two vehicles of communication and information, each of which has been revolutionary for its time.

3. Because of the publication of the King James Version of the Bible, people could now understand the stories inside for themselves. One of these stories is the famous parable of the good Samaritan, told by Jesus in Luke 10:30–35.

   The King James Version shows the way English sounded in 1611. Read the parable first in this version:

And Jesus answering said, A certain man went down from Jerusalem to Jericho, and fell among thieves, which stripped him of his raiment, and wounded him, and departed, leaving him half dead. And by chance there came down a certain priest that way: and when he saw him, he passed by on the other side. And likewise a Levite, when he was at the place, came and looked on him, and passed by on the other side. But a certain Samaritan, as he journeyed, came where he was: and when he saw him, he had compassion on him, And went to him, and bound up his wounds, pouring in oil and wine, and set him on his own beast, and brought him to an inn, and took care of him. And on the morrow when he departed, he took out two pence, and gave them to the host, and said unto him, Take care of him; and whatsoever thou spendest more, when I come again, I will repay thee.

Now also read it in the contemporary version known as *THE MESSAGE*:

Jesus answered by telling a story. 'There was once a man travelling from Jerusalem to Jericho. On the way he was attacked by robbers. They took his clothes, beat him up, and went off leaving him half-dead. Luckily, a priest was on his way down the same road, but when he saw him he angled across to the other side. Then a Levite religious man showed up; he also avoided the injured man. A Samaritan travelling the road came on him. When he saw the man's condition, his heart went out to him. He gave him first aid, disinfecting and bandaging his wounds. Then he lifted him on to his donkey, led him to an inn, and made him comfortable. In the morning he took out two silver coins and gave them to the innkeeper, saying, "Take good care of him. If it costs any more, put it on my bill—I'll pay you on my way back."'

How do the two versions compare? The impact of THE MESSAGE will give you some idea of how the King James Version first sounded to the people of 1611. This inspired people to respond to the story for themselves.

Using the Internet, do a search on 'good Samaritan' for artwork, charitable organisations, music and churches that have been inspired by those who read and understood this story in the English language.

Reproduced with permission from *The People's Bible* published by BRF 2010 (978 1 84101 852 2) www.barnabasinschools.org.uk

Why did it take so long?

Until the 16th century in the Western church, the language of the Bible was Latin (translated from the earlier Greek). Some of our earliest handwritten Bibles, such as the Book of Kells in Ireland, the Lindisfarne Gospels from Holy Island off the coast of Northumberland, and the Winchester Bible, which can still be viewed in that cathedral city, were all in Latin.

These early manuscripts are beautifully and colourfully illustrated and, of course, copied out painstakingly by hand because printing had not yet been invented. However, Latin was the specialist religious language of the church and of the Christian faith and was not accessible to the majority of ordinary people. So why did it take so long for the Bible to be translated into English?

There are several possible reasons:

- Most people could not read or write, so there was no urgency to make the Bible available in everyday English.
- Until the invention of the printing press, there was no easy way to produce copies of a book in large quantities for distribution to a mass audience.
- It was felt that keeping the Bible in Latin or Greek was the best way to preserve the tradition and continuity of the Christian faith. These were the languages in which the first Christians, in the early centuries of the church, had read their Bibles, so Latin and Greek served as an important link with the age from which the story had come. St Jerome had translated the Bible into Latin in the fourth century and this version became known as the Vulgate (which interestingly means 'the people's version', because Latin was the language of the people at that time).
- It was also a case of a 'power game' for some people. The clergy and the educated had learned Latin as well as Greek and they clearly felt that it was best for them to keep the story under their control, rather than letting it get into the hands of ordinary people, who could, they reasoned, potentially upset the 'proper of order of things' under God. Those who could read were the 'go-betweens', mediating the Bible to the masses.

- For ordinary people, who couldn't read, some stories from the Bible were made accessible through statues of saints and Bible characters in churches, carvings on standing crosses or depictions in stained-glass windows. This was another reason not to bother supplying a written version.
- Finally, there were already some popular retellings of parts of the Bible in English, and the church felt that this was all that the majority of people needed. These retellings included some in folk poetry, and there were also paraphrases of key stories, many of which were used in the popular Mystery or Miracle Plays. These plays were a form of Christian street theatre in their day, associated with festivals and performed in many cathedral cities across Britain.

Despite all this, there were a few attempts to put parts of the Bible into contemporary English before the 16th century. The earliest of these that still exists is part of a song composed by Caedmon, who worked near the Abbey of Whitby in the north-east of Britain in the seventh century. The story goes that he was inspired by God to sing of the beginning of creation.

The Venerable Bede, Abbot at Jarrow (also in the north-east), who wrote *The Ecclesiastical History of the English People* in the eighth century, is also said to have begun a translation of John's Gospel in the last years of his life. King Alfred, who was one of Britain's early and very highly educated kings, translated some of the Psalms.

In the early Middle Ages, poems with quotes from the Latin Bible translated into English did exist, in, for example, the works entitled *Piers Ploughman*, *The Dream of the Rood* (all about the cross) and *The Golden Legend* by Caxton. Nevertheless, in the popular mind only a very general outline of the story of the Bible was known and no full English text was produced before the 16th century. The complete story was in the hands of the few. There was little opportunity for people who were ignorant of Latin to gain a better knowledge of the full glory of the Bible's story for themselves.

Activity suggestions

1. Here is a passage from the Vulgate (Latin) version of the Bible, which was the language of all church services and public readings of the Bible for the first 1400 years of its history in Europe. It is the first three verses of Psalm 23.

Dominus regit me, et nihil mihi deerit.
In loco pascuae ibi me collacavit,
super aquam refectionis educavit me;
animam meam convertit.
Deduxit me super semitas justitiae, propter nomen suum.

Biblia Sacra Vulgatae Editionis Rothomagi 1708, Sussex University Library

Compare this with a modern English version of Psalm 23 verses 1–3. (NB: You can look up various translations of passages of the Bible online at www.biblegateway.com. Modern translations include Today's New International Version and the Contemporary English Version.)

- Can you find the Latin for: Lord, green pastures, waters, soul, leads, paths, and name?
- Working from the modern English version, how might you rewrite Psalm 23 in your own language? For example: 'The Lord is my football team captain…'

It's impossible to overestimate the influence of Latin on the whole of European language and culture. Indeed, Latin is still alive and well in the church today. You can find Latin quotes linked to some of the Psalms sung in churches and above the text of some hymns. It is even possible, in some places, still to experience a whole service sung and said in Latin.

Does your school have any Latin words used anywhere, perhaps in a motto or as part of an inscription? When you visit a local

Reproduced with permission from *The People's Bible* published by BRF 2010 (978 1 84101 852 2) www.barnabasinschools.org.uk

church, be on the lookout for any Latin words, maybe on a tombstone. Even our coins still have Latin on them: use the Internet to discover what the abbreviations D.G. REG. F.D. mean.

The Christian community of Taizé in France today often uses Latin texts for its contemporary songs. Examples are *Laudate Omnes Gentes* ('Let all people praise') and *Dona Nobis Pacem, Domine* ('Lord , grant us peace'). Check out www.taize.fr/en.

- Why do you think the leaders of the church were unwilling for so long to abandon Latin?
- Do you think perhaps it helps to worship a mysterious God if a mysterious language is used?

2. Look on the Internet at the British Library's 'Sacred' collection of online texts or in a library for information about the Book of Kells, the Lindisfarne Gospel or the Winchester Bible. Look at a sample page, noting the special writing, the colours and the intricate patterns and drawings that are used to embellish the text.

    Why not have go at this yourself? Decide on a short Bible passage, copy it out in a special calligraphy-like script (you can find one as a font on your PC) and then decide how you will decorate what you have written.

3. Caedmon's story is a remarkable one. This is how part of it is recorded in Bede's *Ecclesiastical History of the English People*:

There was in the Monastery of this Abbess a certain brother particularly remarkable for the Grace of God, who was wont to make religious verses, so that whatever was interpreted to him out of scripture, he soon after put the same into poetical expressions of much sweetness and humility in English, which was his native language. By his verse the minds of many were often excited to despise the world, and to aspire to heaven.

Reproduced with permission from *The People's Bible* published by BRF 2010 (978 1 84101 852 2) www.barnabasinschools.org.uk

Here is the hymn that he sang:

Now [we] must honour
the guardian of heaven,
the might of the architect,
and his purpose,
the work of the father of glory
—as he, the eternal lord,
established
the beginning of wonders.
He, the holy creator,
first created heaven as a roof
for the children of men.
Then the guardian of mankind,
the eternal lord,
the lord almighty
afterwards appointed
the middle earth,
the lands, for men.

Caedmon was just an ordinary herdsman who felt that God had spoken to him and asked him to become a singer. Hilda the Abbess recognised his talent and gave him his big break! He became a monk and it is said that he composed a large number of poems in English, based on Bible passages.

- What do you think it means that Caedmon felt he was inspired by God?
- What do you find interesting about this story?
- What do you think this story has to tell us about the power of putting the Bible into our own language?
- Compare Caedmon's song with the opening verses of Genesis chapter 1.

4. Make a web search, looking for references to the English Mystery or Miracle Plays. Where did they take place? Where do they still take place today? What stories did they cover? Why do you think they were so popular?

A well-written modern novel for children that explores Mystery Plays is *A Little Lower than the Angels* by Geraldine McCaughrean (OUP, 2003). It is the story of a young boy who ends up playing an angel in a mystery play that travels the country, with all the adventures that would have happened during the early Middle Ages.

3

The battle of the books

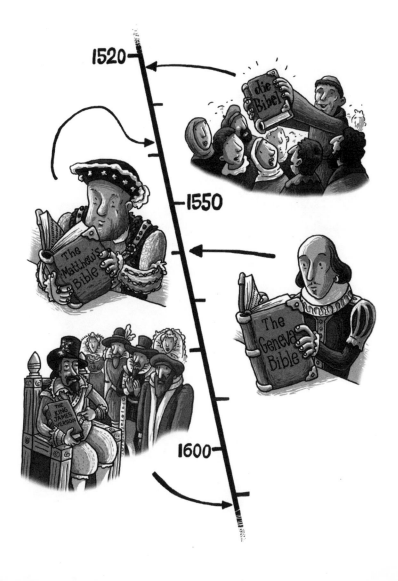

1520

1550

1600

Towards the end of the Middle Ages, Europe began to experience the stirrings of revolt against the Christian church, which was at that time centred on and run from Rome. This happened at first because of the growing corruption in some of the church's practices, and later because of its teachings. Reform movements began to grow in strength and eventually became the Protestant Reformation. Alongside this reform, there grew a renewed interest in the study of the Bible. However, for study to happen effectively, the Bible needed to be translated into the language of the people.

The first English translation of major parts of scripture is known as the Lollard Bible, and is associated with John Wycliffe, who declared that it was 'the right of every man, learned or ignorant, to examine the Bible for himself'. One feature of this translation was that it began to break away from a literal rendering of the Latin and used instead English idioms, English word order and colloquial expressions. Although the distribution of this Bible was suppressed by both the church and the state authorities, it continued to circulate and inspire others.

At this time, Europe was also experiencing the Renaissance—a rediscovery of classical art and literature—and at the same time the printing press had been invented, which led to an explosion in the production of new books. All these changes also opened up access to the original Greek and Hebrew texts of the Bible. Now translators could go back to these sources rather than going via the Latin for their translations. Luther, the hero and herald of the Protestant Reformation, published his German translation of the whole Bible in 1522.

In England, William Tyndale took up the battle to put the stories of the Bible into the hands of ordinary men and women. He was determined that 'the boy that drove the plough should know the scriptures' but, like others before him, he was forced to do his work secretly and abroad for fear of imprisonment. Nevertheless, he was spied upon and later captured and burned at the stake because of his work. Tyndale's last prayer was 'Lord, open the King of England's eyes.' Two years later, Henry VIII authorised the first official translation of the Bible into English. William's prayer had been answered. Copies of his translation did survive and the influence of the language he used was enormous. For example, Tyndale first created the word 'Jehovah' to express the unpronounceable name of God as it is recorded in the Hebrew scriptures, and also the term 'The Living God', which is still widely used by Christians today.

- Next, Miles Coverdale took up the battle and, in 1535, brought together several partial translations to produce the first complete Bible in English. By now England was on the brink of breaking with the power of Rome and the Catholic Church, following the political and religious differences between the Pope and Henry VIII. One result of this was that many new and improved translations of the Bible now began to appear. In 1537 came *The Matthew's Bible*. This version was used by Henry VIII and so, in effect, it was the first official 'authorised Bible'. It drew on numerous earlier versions.
- In 1539 came *Taverner's Bible*.
- Also in 1539 came the first edition of *The King's Bible*, also known as *The Great Bible*, which was appointed to be used in churches throughout the land. These Bibles had to be chained up to prevent people stealing them. Sometimes, worshippers in services would make trouble by clustering round the Bible in church to read it instead of listening to the sermon.
- In 1560 came *The Geneva Bible*—the work of English translators abroad, who had fled to Switzerland to avoid persecution under Queen Mary. This Bible was dedicated to Elizabeth I and was read and used by William Shakespeare. The Geneva Bible was nicknamed *The Breeches Bible* because of its translation of Genesis 3:21, which records how God, having expelled Adam and Eve from the garden of Eden, showed mercy and made for them 'breeches' to cover their nakedness.
- In 1568 came *The Bishop's Bible*, which was a revision of the Great Bible.

Many of these Bibles had woodcut illustrations in between the texts. One version (for King Henry VIII) showed King David looking remarkably like King Henry!

Finally it was agreed to standardise all these different translations, drawing on the best scholarship from each; and so in 1611, in the reign of King James I, came *The King James Bible*, also known as *The Authorised Version*. It follows the Bishop's Bible closely, but much that is best in this final version can be traced right back to William Tyndale.

Activity suggestions

1. Compare the following two early English versions of Psalm 23: 1–3 with a modern English version of the same verses. (NB: You can look up various modern translations of passages of the Bible online at www.biblegateway.com.)

By John Wycliffe:

The Lord gouerneth me, and no thing to me shal lacke; in the place of leswe where he me ful sette. Ouer watir of fulfilling he nurshide me; my soule he conuertide. He bro3te doun me vpon the sties of ri3twisn esse; for his name.

By Miles Coverdale:

The Lorde is my shepherde, I can want nothing.
He fedeth me in a greene pasture,
and ledeth me to a fresh water.
He quickeneth my soule, & bringeth me forth in the ways of righteousness for his names sake.

Reproduced with permission from *The People's Bible* published by BRF 2010 (978 1 84101 852 2) www.barnabasinschools.org.uk

- Which words can you find in both versions?
- Which version has the strangest words for us today?
- Which words in these versions are still used today?
- Can you work out the meanings of: leswe? nurshide? quickeneth? sties?
- Which version do you like the most, and why?

2. Using the Internet or researching in the library, find out more about the early translators: John Wycliffe, Miles Coverdale, William Tyndale and Martin Luther. Share what you have found with others and try to work out how each one contributed to the eventual publication of the King James Version in 1611.

   What do you think inspired these men to risk their lives and face such great opposition—even death itself—to make sure the Bible was available in English for ordinary people to read?

3. William Tyndale has been called the 'hidden father of the English language' because his translation of the Bible made English respectable, formalising a whole range of written spellings and speech patterns for the first time. Before him, English translations were based on second-best translations from the Latin. He also changed the way people thought about their faith in God by enabling them to hear the scriptures in their own language. The King James Version uses about 85 per cent of Tyndale's translation, and some say that the other 15 per cent isn't as good as Tyndale's!

   Find out as much as you can about Tyndale's life. His work was crucial to the development of the King James Version. Focus on finding out what motivated him and why he was prepared to face a martyr's death for what he believed.

   Here are some specific activities based on Tyndale's life and work:

- Books can be dangerous, because they are full of ideas—and people do things when they get ideas. Suppose you were in charge of a country and wanted to stop a book from being

Reproduced with permission from *The People's Bible* published by BRF 2010 (978 1 84101 852 2) www.barnabasinschools.org.uk

read. How would you do it? Write a persuasive argument for or against the idea that books should be accessible for all people. This argument can be extended to include discussion of Internet use and censorship.

- Create a 'Wanted' poster for William Tyndale, also offering a reward for information that would lead to the arrest of anyone reading his Bible.
- The Bible has been likened to a two-edged sword (Hebrews 4:12), a lamp (Psalm 119:105) and a hammer (Jeremiah 23:29). Why do you think these images were chosen? Use these ideas to create calligrams (where the letters of the words 'Holy Bible' are distorted to look like the shapes of some of these images).
- Design a logo for Tyndale's translation of the Bible, incorporating two ideas: that it is very dangerous, and that it is about giving people a new way into the Bible for themselves. Also design the sleeve jacket and write the book blurb.
- Here is Tyndale's version of part of 1 Corinthians 13, which is a hymn about love:

Though I speake with the tonges of men and angels
and yet had no love
I were even as soundynge brass:
and as a tynklynge Cynball.
And though I coulde prophesy and understode all secretes
and all knowledge:
Yee, if I had all fayth so that I coulde move mountayns
oute of there places
And yet had no love, I were nothynge.

Compare this with a modern version (go to www.biblegateway.com). These verses are often read at weddings. Consider how Tyndale has used the poetry of dramatic contrasts to describe the importance of love. Can you see and hear the words in your imagination?

4. Go the following website to see an example of the Bible in Tyndale's translation:
www.bl.uk/onlinegallery/sacredtexts/tyndale.html.

Imagine a Christian lucky (and rich!) enough to own one of Tyndale's new English translations of the Bible. Where do you think they would have kept it safe? If the authorities came looking to confiscate the Bible, where do you think they would hide it?

Draw thought bubbles to show the thoughts that might have gone through a Christian's mind when asked if they had a Bible in English. Would they own up and face the consequences?

4

The book of explosive ideas

The publication of the King James Version in 1611 meant that the words of the Bible were now available to everyone in the contemporary English of the day. The People's Bible had exploded on to the world! Its publication set in motion a chain of events that would change individuals, communities, nations and even, in time, the whole world.

Although there had already been English translations available before this, particularly in the previous hundred years, nevertheless the officially approved, regally sanctioned and state-promoted King James (Authorised) Version opened the floodgates. Now anybody anywhere could hear and understand the stories of the Christians' special book, and this turned everything upside down.

Already, in the 16th century, the Bible in English had ignited change. It had helped people to see that they didn't need the church or the king to tell them what to believe. Now that lots of people had the opportunity to read this book, or hear it read, in their own language, they also discovered that kings can sometimes be wrong. So when they got a king who thought he couldn't do anything wrong because God had made him king, there were bound to be consequences. In the 17th century, more and more people asked questions like 'Who should really be in charge?' and 'Do we even need a king?' Unfortunately, King Charles I didn't really understand what was going on. He believed in the 'divine right of kings' to do exactly what he wanted, and disagreements with Parliament about this finally led to the English Civil War in 1642. Although the king believed that the Bible supported his position, it provided plenty of ammunition for his enemies, who started by questioning his actions and, in the end, cut off his head. Biblical ideas had changed the way people saw the world.

Having the Bible available for individuals and groups to read also opened up new understandings of scripture. They read, for example, that Jesus never founded 'a church' as such and that his first followers wrote about 'the priesthood of all believers'. Church power did not need, it seemed, to reside in the hands of a few trained professionals; anyone could be inspired by God's Spirit to lead and guide a congregation. So new denominations sprang up, organising themselves on these spiritual and democratic principles. They objected to the existing structures of the Church of England and were therefore called 'dissenters'. The state church clamped down on these believers, so many of them decided to seek a new life and to start a Christian utopia in the New World. In 1621 some of them set out westward in a ship called the Mayflower and became the founding fathers of the State of America; this was, to a large degree, because the Bible could now be read by all in English.

Other groups were formed with different understandings of baptism, about the need for bishops to govern the church, and about the ways in which the Holy Spirit inspired worship. For example, in the middle of the 17th century, the Society of Friends was founded, also called Quakers, who read for themselves in the Bible about God's passion for justice in society and how all people everywhere should be treated with respect and dignity. As a result, many of them stood up against unfair practices in business and against laws that disadvantaged the poor and the weak in society.

Others found themselves questioning the received understandings of some Christian doctrines, and so were moved to study the scriptures again for themselves. It was while doing just this that the brothers Charles and John Wesley came to a new understanding of how much God loved them, and this filled them with joy and a passion to share their faith. They took their message out on to the streets and into the countryside of Great Britain, preaching the good news of the gospel to ordinary workers. They set up small classes everywhere, in which the new converts could study the scriptures for themselves. So it was that the Methodist Church was formed. Charles and John Wesley also took the words they read in the Bible and turned them into poetry, setting the words to the popular tunes of the day. Some historians say that this revival, during the 18th century, prevented England from falling into the despair of revolution that gripped the rest of Europe at this time. Again, all this happened because the Bible was available in the people's language.

Enslaved Africans, such as Samuel Sharpe and Olaudah Equiano, read in the Bible about the equality of all people before God, and were empowered to begin their own personal campaigns to abolish the slave trade. Biblical ideas informed Quaker opposition to the trade, and later influenced notable researchers and campaigners, such as Thomas Clarkson and then William Wilberforce, who forced the debate in Parliament. After many years, the abolition of slavery in the British Empire was finally achieved against entrenched political and financial opposition—but the world's first 'popular' political campaign had been fuelled by a biblical idea that continues to affect the whole world.

It was also because Christians could now read the Bible for themselves that they discovered that Jesus had chosen the ordinary workmen of his day to be disciples. Missionary work was not, it seemed, just for professional monks or clergyman. Anyone could be called, and so, during the 18th and 19th centuries, an army of people set sail to take the gospel 'to the ends of the earth'. It was in this period that many missionary societies were formed. It was because these people now read their Bibles that they wanted to take its story to other nations. With the Bible, they also brought health care and education, and a passion to help the poor and disadvantaged in every society in obedience to what they had read.

These stories might seem light years away from today's world, where, although Bibles are freely available, they are often left unread. However, the big ideas like those found in the Bible can spread among people like a fire spreading through a forest, as long as the conditions are right. The Bible is packed with big ideas waiting to be found, and every few years a new one breaks out. One of the latest big ideas has been the 'Drop the Debt' campaign, which protests about the injustice of poorer countries owing such huge amounts of money to the richer ones that they are impossible to pay back. This comes directly from the 'Year of Jubilee' idea found in the Bible in Leviticus 25:8–17.

Activity suggestions

1. Research the following historical themes that relate to this part of the story so far: Charles I and the Divine Right of Kings; the English Civil War; The Pilgrim Fathers; The Quakers; The Wesleys; the Methodist Church; Samuel Sharpe, Olaudah Equiano, Thomas Clarkson, William Wilberforce and the abolition of the slave trade; the Church Mission Society.

2. One of the most successful campaigns of those involved in the movement to abolish the transatlantic slave trade was the Sugar Boycott. In 1791 the Society of Friends (Quakers) distributed leaflets encouraging the public, and especially women, not to buy or use sugar produced in the West Indies by slaves. As a result, about 300,000 people boycotted sugar and sales began to drop. In an effort to increase sales, some shops stocked only sugar imported from India, which had not been produced by slaves, and goods were labelled accordingly. This is similar to the Fair Trade movement today.

   • Where do you think these Quaker Christians found their inspiration to work for international justice like this? Look up the following Bible verses about God's concern for social justice to find out: Isaiah 58:6–7; Amos 8:4–6; Matthew 23:23–24.
   • What images of justice can you find in these Bible passages? What do these Bible verses urge readers to do?

3. It has been said that, even if the Bible were to be lost, much of its content could be recovered from the language of Charles Wesley's hymns. He used a wealth of biblical imagery and he quotes phrases from the King James Version, which would have been his working Bible and inspiration. He uses passages from every book in the New Testament, his favourites being Philippians

Reproduced with permission from *The People's Bible* published by BRF 2010 (978 1 84101 852 2)   www.barnabasinschools.org.uk

chapter 2, Ephesians 3 and 6, Romans 8 and Revelation 5, all of which contain early examples of Christian hymns.

Here are two verses from one of his well-known hymns that are still sung today. Can you make the links between the words of the hymn and Mark 4:35–41 and Psalm 91:1–6?

Jesus, lover of my soul,
Let me to Thy bosom fly,
While the nearer waters roll,
While the tempest still is high!
Hide me, O my Saviour, hide,
Till the storm of life be past;
Safe into the haven guide,
Oh, receive my soul at last!

Other refuge have I none,
Hangs my helpless soul on Thee;
Leave, ah! leave me not alone,
Still support and comfort me!
All my trust on Thee is stayed,
All my help from Thee I bring;
Cover my defenceless head
With the shadow of Thy wing.

4. Here is an assembly outline and ideas for classroom follow-up on the life of William Wilberforce and the abolition of the slave trade: www.barnabasinschools.org.uk/3285.

5. A colony in the part of West Africa now known as Sierra Leone was set up by the Clapham Sect (a group of evangelical Christians who met to study the Bible together). It was to be a place where the freed slaves could go to and live in peace. This group had also founded the Church Mission Society in 1799 and they decided that the CMS should begin its first work in Africa there. The first missionaries were sent to set up schools, churches

and medical care for the ex-slave community. The journey from Great Britain could take anything from two to seven months, depending on the weather. Sadly, many missionaries died in service after only a few years in a foreign climate. Comparatively few women missionaries went out in the early days of the CMS but, at a town called Charlotte in Sierra Leone, a school was run by Mary Beale for almost 30 years. Mary Ann Coke is, however, credited as being the first CMS woman missionary. She worked in Calcutta from 1822. Through the work of missionaries like these, the stories of the Bible were taken all around the world.

- Why do you think the first CMS missionaries volunteered to go to Africa? You might like to look up the following Bible verses in order to explain their reasons for taking up this challenge: Matthew 28:18–20; John 3:16; Romans 15:20–21.
- You can find out more about CMS today at www.cms-uk.org.
- Imagine that the date is 1820 and your best friend has decided to apply to go out with CMS to Africa. Write a letter to him or her, explaining what you think of the idea. You can decide to be either in favour of or against the plan.

Reproduced with permission from *The People's Bible* published by BRF 2010 (978 1 84101 852 2) www.barnabasinschools.org.uk

5

The book that shaped a language

I t is impossible to overestimate the impact of the publication of the King James Version in 1611. For the first time, here was a book in English that was being either read or heard by almost all the population of these islands. This helped people to appreciate the true potential of their own native tongue, as well as giving them access to a greater range of expressions when they spoke it. It wasn't just the ideas in the Bible that transformed people's lives; it was the language of the translation itself. Its influence began to be felt everywhere.

For example, there were many new words that appeared for the first time in this Bible. A number of them were first coined by William Tyndale, on whose earlier translation of the Bible the King James Version so largely depended. These words were not necessarily invented by Tyndale, but when he put them in the Bible it meant that they came into general usage. They include: longsuffering, peacemakers, beautiful, landlady, taskmaster, viper, seashore, stumbling block, fisherman, open-hearted, scapegoat, clear-eyed and broken-hearted.

In addition, there were many everyday expressions of speech that became well known and loved because of the publication of the King James Bible. Some of these phrases live on today and are used by people who don't even realise that they come straight from this Bible. They include: casting pearls before swine; the eleventh hour; love as strong as death; the seven pillars of wisdom; how are the mighty fallen; your treasure is where your heart is; eat, drink and be merry; am I my brother's keeper?; let there be light; the Spirit is willing but the flesh is weak; a man after my own heart; a land flowing with milk and honey; filthy lucre; the powers that be; O ye of little faith!; a two-edged sword.

The King James Version of the Bible also sorted out a great many English spellings and made the English language respectable. Until this time, people tended to spell English words in any way they liked. For the first time, most of the country could share in one edition of a book—and that led to some spellings being 'fixed'. So, thanks to the King James Version, 'wen' became 'when'; 'mought' became 'mouth'; 'thers' became 'theirs'; 'moost' became 'most'; 'burthen' became 'burden'.

The words and phrases of the Bible became so well known through the King James Version that they influenced generations of poets, writers and artists, many of whom were Christians and used the Bible in their works. It has been said that it is impossible fully to appreciate the literary heritage of Great Britain without knowledge of the Bible and, in particular, without a knowledge of the words of the King James Version, which shaped so much of that heritage.

Great English poets such as George Herbert, Henry Vaughan and, later, William Wordsworth all drew on biblical words and themes, which they had first learned from the King James Version. Likewise, the leading Christian hymn writers of the 18th century, such as Charles Wesley, Isaac Watts and Augustus Toplady, lifted whole phrases from the King James Version to put into their songs, which also meant that its language became part of Britain's heritage.

Others, like the writer Lord Byron, whose dashing lifestyle captured the nation's interest at the beginning of the 19th century, also knew the King James Version well—if only, at times, to react against its influence and especially against some of its more sombre passages about sin and judgment. However, Byron happily used biblical word-pictures in 'The Vision of Judgement' to satirise the life and death of King George III.

In the 19th century, too, it was not uncommon for those who went to school to be given huge chunks of the King James Version to be learnt off by heart. It was felt that this would not only improve a child's morals but also give him or her the tools to speak English well. John Ruskin wrote this about the language of the King James Version of the Bible:

It lives on the ear like music that can never be forgotten—like the sound of a church bell, which a convert hardly knows he can forgo... It is part of the national mind and the anchor of national seriousness. The dower of all the gifts and trials of a man's life is hidden beneath its words. It is the representative of the best moments. There is not a Protestant with a spark of righteousness about him whose spiritual biography is not his English Bible.

FROM *FORS CLAVIGERA*, LETTER 76

In our own day, the former Poet Laureate Andrew Motion wrote this in 2009: 'All children should be taught the Bible… Without its great stories, they cannot hope to understand history and literature.'

Christians call the Bible 'the word of God', and for four centuries that word has been identified with the language of the King James Version. The power of its language has been, for many people, the very voice of God. The Bible is still most often quoted in this version, even by those who do not go to church and would not say that they are committed Christians.

Activity suggestions

1. Printed below are the Ten Commandments as written in the King James Version. Passages like this would have been learned off by heart and were also often written up on the walls of churches.

   And God spake all these words, saying,
   I am the LORD thy God, which have brought thee out of the land of Egypt, out of the house of bondage.
   Thou shalt have no other gods before me.
   Thou shalt not make unto thee any graven image, or any likeness of any thing that is in heaven above, or that is in the earth beneath, or that is in the water under the earth.
   Thou shalt not bow down thyself to them, nor serve them: for I the LORD thy God am a jealous God, visiting the iniquity of the fathers upon the children unto the third and fourth generation of them that hate me;
   And shewing mercy unto thousands of them that love me, and keep my commandments.

Thou shalt not take the name of the LORD thy God in vain;
for the LORD will not hold him guiltless that taketh his name
in vain.
Remember the sabbath day, to keep it holy.
Six days shalt thou labour, and do all thy work:
But the seventh day is the sabbath of the LORD thy God:
in it thou shalt not do any work, thou, nor thy son, nor thy
daughter, thy manservant, nor thy maidservant, nor thy
cattle, nor thy stranger that is within thy gates:
For in six days the LORD made heaven and earth, the sea,
and all that in them is, and rested the seventh day: wherefore
the LORD blessed the sabbath day, and hallowed it.
Honour thy father and thy mother: that thy days may be long
upon the land which the LORD thy God giveth thee.
Thou shalt not kill.
Thou shalt not commit adultery.
Thou shalt not steal.
Thou shalt not bear false witness against thy neighbour.
Thou shalt not covet thy neighbour's house, thou shalt not
covet thy neighbour's wife, nor his manservant, nor his
maidservant, nor his ox, nor his ass, nor any thing that is thy
neighbour's.

Exodus 20:1–17

These were God's top ten rules for life.

- How would you translate these rules into words that are used today? Pick three rules to start with, then try some more.
- Many of them are in the form of what people should *not* do. Can you reword them, stressing the positive each time?
- What would be your top ten rules for a safe and happy world?
- Can you make a poster of the Ten Commandments to hang up on the wall of your classroom?

Reproduced with permission from *The People's Bible* published by BRF 2010 (978 1 84101 852 2)   www.barnabasinschools.org.uk

2. Read the following three verses of a hymn by Isaac Watts (1674–1748), celebrating the Bible. The hymn is full of references to words from the King James Version that Isaac Watts knew. Compare the hymn with Psalm 19 in the King James Version (see www.biblegateway.com). Can you spot which phrases Isaac Watts has borrowed?

The heavens declare Thy glory, Lord,
In every star Thy wisdom shines;
But when our eyes behold Thy Word
We read Thy name in fairer lines.

The rolling sun, the changing light,
And night and day, Thy power confess;
But the blest volume Thou hast writ
Revels Thy justice and Thy grace.

Great Sun of righteousness, arise,
Bless the dark world with heavenly light:
Thy gospel makes the simple wise;
Thy laws are pure, Thy judgements right.

3. Can you devise an acrostic poem to celebrate the Bible, in which each line begins with one of the letters of 'Holy Bible' and expresses something of the impact that the Bible has had on Britain and the world over the past 400 years? Use some of the ideas from this section of the booklet. It could start:

Hurrah! *The Bible is now in English*
Open *for anyone to read*

4. Look up and read the stories linked to some of the everyday English phrases that have come down to us through the King James Version. For example:

Reproduced with permission from *The People's Bible* published by BRF 2010 (978 1 84101 852 2) www.barnabasinschools.org.uk

- 'Am I my brother's keeper?': see Genesis 4:1–15, the story of the first murder.
- 'The eleventh hour': see Matthew 20:1–16, a parable of Jesus about the generosity of God.
- 'A man after my own heart': see Acts13:16–25, where Paul is relating the story of God's people and talking of King David.
- 'A two-edged sword': see Hebrews 4:12–13, where God's words are being described.

The website www.crossref-it.info explores English literature and biblical roots. There are further activity suggestions here for teachers to use in the classroom related to the influence of the King James Version on the English language.

Reproduced with permission from *The People's Bible* published by BRF 2010 (978 1 84101 852 2) www.barnabasinschools.org.uk

6

Translation, translation, translation

The publication of the King James Version in 1611 was an important milestone in the story of Bible translation. Although this version became the most commonly used and most widely known English text for over 300 years after that date (and is still the preferred version for many Christians today), it had established an important principle—namely, that the Bible should be available in the everyday language of ordinary people.

Towards the end of the 19th century, revisions and new translations began to appear. Biblical scholarship had been given a boost by the discovery of older and more reliable Greek and Hebrew texts of the original books of the Bible, and this led to the Revised Version in 1881 and then the full Revised Standard Version in 1952. Each time, the aim was to produce a more accurate translation of the Bible, although there was often a struggle to balance that aim with a concern to retain the poetry and grandeur of expression that many people felt had been a characteristic of the King James Version.

Throughout the 20th century and up to the present day, the translation process has continued apace, each new version trying to be more rigorously accurate as well as readable for the person on the street. Of course, the English language has changed over 400 years. No longer do we use 'thee' and 'thou' in our everyday speech, and other words and expressions in common usage in 1611 have since fallen obsolete. For example, we no longer use words like 'agues', 'peradventure', 'tares', 'emerods' (see 1 Samuel 5:6 in the King James Version) or the term 'begat'.

Today an abundance of Bible versions, retellings, translations, revisions and paraphrases is available to readers. In addition, the text layout and supporting illustrations have changed as new printing possibilities have become available. All this is designed to attract new readers to open this most important of books, so that it might impact lives today just as it did in 1611. There are youth Bibles, children's Bibles, Manga Bibles, an Amplified Bible, a Living Bible and the paraphrase version called THE MESSAGE, whose freshness of expression can remind us just how the King James Version must have sounded to its first readers.

Nevertheless, some Christians feel that much has been lost from the King James Version in these modern translations. The King James Version was produced at about the same time as Shakespeare was writing his later plays, and the language therefore represents a distillation of all that was considered best in English at that time. Many people argue that there is a majesty and poetry in the language of the King James Version that lends a proper dignity to such an important a book. They feel that the story of God's work in the world, and the words of Jesus, need cadences and rhythms that sound as if they come from the pen of a great poet rather than remaining at the mercy of the scholarly translators, with their prosaic accuracy. As we have seen in a previous chapter, the influence of many words and phrases used in the King James Version has lasted, and many are still in use in English today. Shakespearean English is still read, appreciated, performed and enjoyed, so why shouldn't that also be true for the King James Version of the Bible?

Another effect of the availability of the Bible in contemporary English in 1611 was that Christians realised that other people around the world had the right to read the scriptures in their own languages. Organisations such as Wycliffe Bible Translators and Bible Society have been at the forefront of translating and distributing the Bible in thousands of languages, even in some spoken by relatively small numbers of people. This enormous task is ongoing and there are still some people groups who have access only to parts of the Bible in their own language.

Translation is not just about the words, however well chosen they are. A key verse in the Bible for Christians is found in John 1:14, which says (in the Contemporary English Version), 'The Word became a human being and lived here with us.' Christians believe that God 'translated' himself into the flesh and blood of Jesus, so that the rest of the world could know what God is like. Likewise, Christians are called to translate the stories and truths of the Bible by the way they live, in order to show others what the Bible calls us all to be and become. In this way, the people of the world can 'read the Bible' for themselves without even picking up the book. Christians are meant to be living translations of the Bible. Paul wrote as much in 2 Corinthians 3:3: 'You are like a letter written by Christ... not written with pen and ink... [but] by the Spirit of the living God' (CEV).

However, for this to happen, it is vital that everyone one can read and hear the Bible's story for themselves in their own language. In this way they can absorb and commit themselves to its truths in order to become Christ's letters for the world around.

Activity suggestions

1. Go to the website www.biblegateway.com and type in any Bible reference you like (that is, the name of the Bible book, the chapter number and the verse number). Try, for example, John 3:16 or Genesis 3:3. Then click on the various possible translations to see how many different versions you can find. Print some of them out and compare the variety of ways in which your verse has been expressed in English. You can also look up verses in other languages at the same website.

   - Which version do you like the best and why?
   - Which version sounds the most poetic and special?
   - Which version do you find the easiest to understand?
   - Which one would you prefer to try to memorise?

2. Read the King James Version of the song that Mary sings in Luke 1:46–55, in which she expresses her joy that God has chosen her to be the mother of Jesus. This song is still sung today in many churches, and in this very version.

   And Mary said, My soul doth magnify the Lord,
   And my spirit hath rejoiced in God my Saviour.
   For he hath regarded the low estate of his handmaiden:

Reproduced with permission from *The People's Bible* published by BRF 2010 (978 1 84101 852 2) www.barnabasinschools.org.uk

for, behold, from henceforth all generations shall call
me blessed.
For he that is mighty hath done to me great things;
and holy is his name.
And his mercy is on them that fear him from generation
to generation.
He hath shewed strength with his arm; he hath scattered the
proud in the imagination of their hearts.
He hath put down the mighty from their seats, and exalted
them of low degree.
He hath filled the hungry with good things; and the rich he
hath sent empty away.
He hath holpen his servant Israel, in remembrance of
his mercy;
As he spake to our fathers, to Abraham, and to his seed
for ever.

- Why do you think that some people today prefer this version?
- What do you like or dislike about it?
- What do you find strange or attractive about these words?

3. Translating the Bible into another language is a demanding task. It isn't just about getting the words right. It is also about the meaning of the words and finding the appropriate local idioms and images that will make sense within the culture of those who will be using the new version. The Bible was originally written at a different time and within a culture quite alien to many people today.

   For example, read the famous story of Daniel and the lions' den in Daniel 6. This story might seem simple to translate, but think about a version for an Inuit audience—that is, the indigenous people of northern Canada and Alaska, who may never have seen a lion, let alone a lions' den. How could you translate it for them?

   There are some challenging translation puzzles available on

Reproduced with permission from *The People's Bible* published by BRF 2010 (978 1 84101 852 2)   www.barnabasinschools.org.uk

the Wycliffe Bible Translators website, which will give you a flavour of their work.

Go to http://wycliffe.org.uk/live/foryou/games.html and try to solve the puzzles.

4. The words of the Lord's Prayer (see Matthew 6:9–13) are very special for Christians, particularly in the King James Version. Go to www.biblegateway.com and type in the Bible reference above to obtain the King James Version words of this prayer). Even so, many of the words used are not in common usage today because language has changed.

Can you produce a new version of your own, which uses words and phrases that are part of your everyday speech? For some ideas to help with this, go to www.barnabasinschools.org.uk/2621.

Reproduced with permission from *The People's Bible* published by BRF 2010 (978 1 84101 852 2) www.barnabasinschools.org.uk

7

What's so special about the Bible?

The year 2011 marks the 400th anniversary of the publication of the King James Version—an event that, as we have seen, had a huge impact not only on the history of the Church but also on the development of the culture of Great Britain and, through its empire and missions, on the whole world. But of course there have been many thousands of books published in English since then, so what is so special about the Bible?

Pick up a copy of the King James Version and, as you hold it, stop to think for a moment about what you have in your hands. This is not just one book but a whole library of 66 books, compiled over hundreds of years, containing history, poetry, advice, letters and biography within its pages. It has been said that the Bible is 'the source book of Western civilisation' (D.H. Lawrence), meaning that some of the biggest ideas about who we are and how we are to live started in here. It's the single most important book for Christians; Muslims treat it as a holy book, and the Jews' own Hebrew scriptures make up the first part of the Bible, known to Christians as the Old Testament.

Christians believe that this book is not just another collection of writings from long ago but an inspired collection of unique scriptures, through whose connected story God has revealed his character and purposes to the world. When Christians read this book, they believe that they are opening themselves up to one of the most important ways that God speaks to people today. In its pages they believe that they can discover more about themselves, too, as they read how God worked with individuals and communities from the tribes of Judah and Israel all those years ago. Human nature has not changed, and the insights into God gained by the patriarchs (such as Abraham and Moses), the kings and the prophets of the Old Testament hold true for the 21st-century reader. Even more importantly, the Bible contains the record of the life and ministry of Jesus Christ, alongside the story of how the first Christians spread the faith during the first century AD. Once again, the records of these words, stories and experiences have been the way in which the followers of Jesus Christ in each age have discovered how to live life 'more abundantly', just as Jesus promised.

More than once in his writings, Paul comments that the scriptures (which, for him, meant the Old Testament) are an important source of inspiration and encouragement for believers. He writes in 2 Timothy 3:16, 'Everything in the Scriptures is God's Word. All of it is useful for teaching and helping people and for correcting them and showing them how to live' (CEV). Again, in Romans 15:4, he writes, 'And the Scriptures were written to teach and encourage us by giving us hope' (CEV).

Elsewhere, Paul says that his letters should be read out in the churches; and of course the words of Jesus and the stories about him were regularly retold whenever those first small Christian congregations met, scattered as they were across the Roman Empire.

Christians believe that the Bible is not just an important historical document recording the ups and downs of the Hebrew people; nor is it simply an interesting philosophical and moral resource, offering readers uplifting spiritual advice. Christians believe much more—namely, that this remarkable book can make a difference in the lives of the individuals and communities that take it seriously. It challenges human priorities and thought patterns with truths about God; it offers guidance and instruction about how best to live lives that are honouring to God; it gives warnings to people whenever they make choices that are harmful to themselves, to others and to the wider world. Most significantly, it brings Christians to a lively experience of the presence of God here and now, which is individually life-changing and can, as we have seen in previous chapters, have a remarkable impact on the world at large. This is why the Bible is special and why Christians believe that it is so important to make it available for people to read in their own languages.

Many individuals have a story to tell about how important the Bible has been for them.

- David Suchet, the British actor who plays Poirot in the Agatha Christie murder dramas, began his journey of faith after he started reading a Bible in a hotel room, while on tour in the USA.
- Dame Cecily Saunders, the founder of the modern hospice movement, began searching for God after seeing the committed faith of her friends. It was while she was on holiday with these friends, and was invited to join them in their Bible studies, that everything suddenly began to make sense and she became a Christian.
- At the end of his life, the American actor Steve McQueen invited evangelist Billy Graham to his home. Steve put his faith in God and asked Billy for a Bible, which he read and treasured during the last days of his life in hospital.
- Kriss Akabusi, a British athlete in the 1980s, came to faith at the Commonwealth Games in Edinburgh when he read a copy of the New Testament left in his hotel room.
- Kaka, the talented Brazilian footballer who makes no secret of his Christian faith, is outspoken about his belief in 'the God of the Bible'. After reading Jesus' words in Matthew 25—that feeding hungry people is like feeding Jesus himself—Kaka became an 'Ambassador against Hunger' on behalf of the World Food Programme of the UN.

Many organisations have made it their aim to do just what the 1611 King James Version did, which is to tell the stories of the Bible in ways that people of the day can understand and to which they can respond. The Bible Reading Fellowship (BRF) does this by producing Bible reading notes and books; it can also be done through programmes that aim to bring the Bible to life with children and families, such as those offered by BRF's Barnabas children's ministry team in churches and schools nationally. For more information, visit www.barnabasinchurches.org.uk and www.barnabasinschools.org.uk.

The story of the translation of the Bible into English may have begun more than 400 years ago, but it continues today in many forms. Christians still believe that this book is special and that putting it into people's hands in their own language can be dynamite, transforming individuals, communities and the whole world for the better.

Activity suggestions

1. Find an assembly outline on 'Images to describe the Bible' at www.barnabasinschools.org.uk/2675.

2. A lesson outline for KS2 on 'Introducing the Bible' can be found at www.barnabasinschools.org.uk/2712.

3. There is a classroom activity on 'The big story of the Bible in mime' at www.barnabasinschools.org.uk/2684.

4. For a classroom activity on 'The books of the Bible', see www.barnabasinschools.org.uk/2685.

5. Find a quiz on the Bible for the classroom or assembly at www.barnabasinschools.org.uk/2687.

6. For an activity exploring how to get around the Bible and work out what is where, visit www.barnabasinschools.org.uk/2688.

Reproduced with permission from *The People's Bible* published by BRF 2010 (978 1 84101 852 2) www.barnabasinschools.org.uk

*But among all our joys, there was no one that more filled our hearts
than the blessed continuance of the preaching of God's sacred Word
among us, which is that inestimable treasure which excelleth all the
riches of earth; because the fruit thereof extendeth itself, not only to the
time spent in this transitory world, but directeth and disposeth men unto
that eternal happiness which is above in heaven.*

EXTRACT FROM THE PREFACE TO THE KING JAMES VERSION OF THE BIBLE
PUBLISHED IN 1611

Story Assemblies for the School Year

36 assemblies with five-minute stories, teacher's notes and RE follow-up

Edward J. Carter

This book is full of memorable stories, designed to engage and delight pupils at primary level. The stories are essentially parables about God and the events in the Bible, creatively told to help children understand the big story of God's love for the world.

There are six themes in total, each with its own easy-to-make storytelling prop. The stories within each theme are divided into six weekly episodes, covering a wide range of contemporary values and topics. Together the stories cover the whole school year, with a key theme and a story in six parts for each half-term period.

As well as being ideal for collective worship, there are practical follow-up ideas to help children connect with the stories in the classroom. The six themes cover:

- God's creation
- The message of the Old Testament prophets
- Stories about Christian values
- The story of Holy Week and Easter
- Jesus' resurrection and ascension
- The journeys of the apostle Paul

ISBN 978 1 84101 699 3   £8.99
Available direct from BRF using the order form on page 63. Alternatively, please visit www.brfonline.org.uk.

Stories for Interactive Assemblies

15 story-based assemblies to get children talking

Nigel Bishop

Collective worship is an ideal time to combine biblical teaching with contemporary storytelling. The 15 stories in this book are all based in the world of the classroom but have their roots in the parables of Jesus. They are designed to stimulate children's thinking and get them talking in the assembly and afterwards in the classroom.

Primary children of all ages will recognise themselves and their classmates in these stories and, even if they do not recognise the original parable, they are invited to relate to its underlying message.

Each story is followed by questions for the assembly or classroom, designed to help the children interact with some of the issues raised, plus suggestions for practical activities, based on different learning styles. Each story also includes:

- A target theme to help direct the teacher towards the main teaching objective
- A prayer or reflection to close the assembly if desired
- Bible references for the original parables
- Information to link the teaching to PSHE/Citizenship and the non-statutory national framework for RE or local SACRE guidelines

ISBN 978 1 84101 465 4   £6.99

Available direct from BRF using the order form on page 63. Alternatively, please visit www.brfonline.org.uk.

The Barnabas Schools' Bible

Including Bible Encyclopedia

Rhona Davies

Illustrated by Marcin Piwowarski

This new Children's Bible includes stories chosen to cover all the main events, retold with a continuous thread.

There are 365 stories, one for every day of the year, each accompanied by Bible quotations from a real Bible translation, giving readers a taste of the language and style of the original texts.

The stylish illustrations illuminate and inform, while the easily accessible encyclopedia at the end of the book helps to explain the context and background of the stories. All combine to make this a useful and readable Bible for older children.

ISBN 978 1 84101 564 4   £12.99
Available direct from BRF using the order form on page 63. Alternatively, please visit www.brfonline.org.uk.

Barnabas RE Days

Exploring Christianity creatively

A Barnabas RE Day is a full day's visit to your school to bring the Bible to life for primary-aged children through a range of the creative arts. The Barnabas children's ministry team explores the themes 'Whose world?', 'Who is my neighbour?', 'Who am I?', 'What's so special about the Bible?', 'It's not fair', Advent and Christmas, Lent and Easter, and Harvest, using Bible stories and contemporary life illustrations. The themes address many PSHE/Citizenship objectives. For example:

- *Whose world?* What improves or harms our environment; responsibility towards our environment.
- *Who is my neighbour?* Recognising choices; realising that other people have needs; caring; bullying; racism.
- *Who am I?* Recognising similarities and differences between people; feeling positive about ourselves; recognising our worth as individuals; recognising and challenging stereotypes.

The sessions use different creative arts according to the particular skills of the team member undertaking your booking, such as storytelling, music, dance, mime, drama, creative writing or drawing. The material is based on biblical and historical accounts, personal story and shared experience.

The timetable, class groupings and themes are completely flexible and will be organised between you and the Barnabas ministry team to suit your school's needs.

A full-day visit costs just £275, of which £50 is placed down as a non-returnable deposit when booking.

For more information, contact the Barnabas Team Administrator on 01865 319704 or email barnabas@brf.org.uk. You can also visit the website: www.barnabasinschools.org.uk.

ORDERFORM

REF	TITLE	PRICE	QTY	TOTAL
699 3	Story Assemblies for the School Year	£8.99		
465 4	Stories for Interactive Assemblies	£6.99		
564 4	The Barnabas Schools' Bible	£12.99		

POSTAGE AND PACKING CHARGES					Postage and packing	
Order value	UK	Europe	Surface	Air Mail	Donation	
£7.00 & under	£1.25	£3.00	£3.50	£5.50	TOTAL	
£7.10–£30.00	£2.25	£5.50	£6.50	£10.00		
Over £30.00	FREE	prices on request				

Name _____ Account Number _____

Address _____

_____ Postcode _____

Telephone Number _____

Email _____

Payment by: ❏ Cheque ❏ Mastercard ❏ Visa ❏ Postal Order ❏ Maestro

Card no ▢▢▢▢ ▢▢▢▢ ▢▢▢▢ ▢▢▢▢ ▨▨▨

Valid from ▢▢▢▢ Expires ▢▢▢▢ Issue no. ▨▨▨

Security code* ▢▢▢ *Last 3 digits on the reverse of the card.
ESSENTIAL IN ORDER TO PROCESS YOUR ORDER

Shaded boxes for Maestro use only

Signature _____ Date _____

All orders must be accompanied by the appropriate payment.

Please send your completed order form to:
BRF, 15 The Chambers, Vineyard, Abingdon OX14 3FE
Tel. 01865 319700 / Fax. 01865 319701 Email: enquiries@brf.org.uk

❏ Please send me further information about BRF publications.

Available from your local Christian bookshop. BRF is a Registered Charity

About
brf:

BRF is a registered charity and also a limited company, and has been in existence since 1922. Through all that we do—producing resources, providing training, working face-to-face with adults and children, and via the web—we work to resource individuals and church communities in their Christian discipleship through the Bible, prayer and worship.

Our Barnabas children's team works with primary schools and churches to help children under 11, and the adults who work with them, to explore Christianity creatively and to bring the Bible alive.

To find out more about BRF and its core activities and ministries, visit:

www.brf.org.uk
www.brfonline.org.uk
www.barnabasinschools.org.uk
www.barnabasinchurches.org.uk
www.messychurch.org.uk
www.foundations21.org.uk

If you have any questions about BRF and our work, please email us at

enquiries@brf.org.uk

enter